The Christmas Menorahs

How a Town Fought Hate

This book is dedicated to
Isaac Schnitzer, Teresa Hanley, and their families,
and to Wayne Inman, Margaret MacDonald, Reverend Keith Torney,
and the other courageous people of Billings,
who've reminded me of the power of goodness. J.C.

For my mother, Gloria. B.F.

The Christmas Menorahs

How a Town Fought Hate

Janice Cohn, D.S.W.

Illustrations by
Bill Farnsworth

Albert Whitman & Company, Morton Grove, Illinois

Introduction

Acts of hatred and prejudice have always been with us. So, too, have individuals who refuse to accept such acts and are determined to resist.

Occasionally, a whole community joins together to fight against bullies and bigots. People act, knowing there is risk, because, quite simply, it is "the right thing to do." This is what happened during the holiday season of 1993, in the town of Billings, Montana.

A stranger walking down Billings's pleasant streets would have no way of knowing that extraordinary things happened there, events which were themselves inspired by people in another place and another time, over half a century ago.

What gives people the courage to fight against hatred and the wisdom to understand just how important that fight is? What causes some communities to draw together when faced with acts of bigotry and violence, while other communities split apart? In Billings, it was a combination of factors, including:

A family who, having been victimized by skinheads, eloquently spoke out and refused to be intimidated.

A police chief who understood the seriousness of hate crimes, even minor ones, and was determined that they would not be tolerated under any circumstances.

A lay church leader who remembered a story she had heard as a child, which she then used to help inspire her community.

Clergy of all faiths who were committed to genuinely practicing what they preached.

A newspaper which sought out and published the truth about local hate crimes and then used its editorial pages to urge the community to take a principled stand.

Town residents, of many different races, religions, and backgrounds, who were willing to fight for a basic value despite threats of violence.

The people of Billings don't consider themselves "heroes" or special or unique in any way. What happened in Billings, they point out, could happen in any town.

Yes . . . any town. And every town. Perhaps someday the children who read this story will remember Billings and use its lessons in their own communities.

Though *The Christmas Menorahs* is strongly based on fact, some of the events have been slightly altered and/or their sequence changed. I believe, however, that I have remained true to the spirit of the story.

The legend of King Christian and the Danes has been told and retold to millions of people since World War II. In fact, the Danish Jews were never ordered to wear the Star of David after the Nazi occupation, in part because there was little anti-Semitism in Denmark, and the Nazis knew the Danes and their good king would never cooperate.

Though King Christian did not ride out of the palace wearing a Jewish star, he always supported the Jewish community. The Danish people themselves took great risks in hiding their Jewish fellow citizens and helping them escape to Sweden in the fall of 1943.

Over the years, this legend, which inspired the citizens of Billings, has made an indelible mark on people's hearts and minds, perhaps because it is about people acting on the highest principle: loving their neighbors as themselves.

The acts of hate in Billings dramatically decreased after the events described in this book. There is, of course, no guarantee that the battle against bigotry will not have to be fought again. But for now, the haters are mostly quiet, aware that they will receive no hospitality from this "ordinary," special town.

Janice Cohn, 1995

6

It was a cold December night in Billings, Montana. Christmas lights twinkled on many houses, and from a few homes, Hanukkah menorahs shone into the darkness.

It was the third night of Hanukkah. At Isaac Schnitzer's house, there was a menorah in almost every window. Isaac was in the den, working on his math homework. Suddenly there was a loud crash.

Isaac jumped up.

Mrs. Davis, the baby-sitter, ran in from the kitchen.

"What happened?" she called. "Are you okay?"

"I'm all right," Isaac answered. "I think the noise came from my bedroom."

Isaac and Mrs. Davis headed down the hall. When they opened the door to Isaac's room, they felt a rush of icy air. Isaac flipped on the light and they saw what had happened.

The big front window was shattered. The electric menorah that had been on the windowsill was lying on the carpet, still glowing. Pieces of glass covered the floor, and on Isaac's bed was a big rock.

"My goodness," exclaimed Mrs. Davis. "Someone threw a rock through your window!"

Isaac rushed to the window and looked outside. The street was quiet. Whoever had thrown the rock was gone.

"Who did it?" Isaac asked. "Why would someone *do* this?"

"I don't know," said Mrs. Davis, shivering. She quickly pulled down the blinds and unplugged the menorah. "Isaac, I think we should call your parents. Let's go to the kitchen and find the phone number they left us."

Isaac nodded. It was very cold in his room, and suddenly he didn't want to be there. What if he had been in bed when the rock came flying through?

A little while later, Isaac's parents came home. When they saw the window, they just stared for a moment. Then they turned to Isaac and folded him in their arms.

"Are you okay?" his dad asked.

"I'm all right," Isaac told them, but he was glad his mom and dad were home.

"It must have been scary, honey," Isaac's mom said softly to her son. She turned to Isaac's dad. "I knew this would happen," she said. "These terrible people kept threatening and threatening..."

"Threatening what?" Isaac asked. "Who's threatening us?"

"Isaac, we'll talk about this in a little while, I promise," his dad told him. "Now your mother and I need to figure out what to do."

"We should call the police right away," Isaac's mom insisted. "Chief Inman will come."

"Wow—Chief Inman's coming? Remember when he came to my school? He's nice," Isaac said.

"Yes, he is," his mom agreed, "and I know that he'll help us. In the meantime, we should leave everything just the way it is."

"You mean, so he can look for clues?" Isaac asked her.

"Exactly," she told him.

Isaac was the first to see Chief Inman as he came up the walk, and he ran to greet him at the door. His parents followed close behind.

"Thank you for coming so quickly," said Isaac's mom.

The police chief was wearing his uniform. Isaac couldn't help staring at the gun in the holster on his belt.

"Isaac, your mom and Mrs. Davis and I need to talk to Chief Inman alone for awhile," his dad told him.

"Aw, Dad," Isaac said, "can't I stay?"

"Not this time," his dad answered. "But we'll call you before Chief Inman leaves."

"Yes," said the chief. "I'll need you to tell me exactly what you heard and saw."

Isaac reluctantly went into the den and tried to do the rest of his math problems. But he just couldn't. Finally, he closed his books, crept down the hall, and listened outside the living room.

He heard his mom say, "We're *not* taking down the Hanukkah decorations. Being Jewish is who we are—we're not going to hide it."

"You shouldn't have to," Chief Inman said, "yet it might be safer. The police will try their best to protect you, but with the holidays here, Jewish families seem to be these haters' special targets, especially families with menorahs in their windows."

"I guess that's their idea of getting in the holiday spirit," Isaac's dad muttered angrily.

"Throwing rocks through a Jewish kid's bedroom window—it's a twisted way of celebrating," Chief Inman said, shaking his head.

When Isaac heard that, he couldn't help rushing into the living room. "Someone threw a rock in my window because I'm *Jewish?*" he asked.

"I think that is why someone threw that rock," Chief Inman answered. "There's a small group of people in Billings who have been causing a lot of trouble. First they sent out leaflets saying hateful things about Jews and some other groups who live here. Then they spray-painted threats and insults on a Native-American home and tried to frighten African-Americans in their church. Last week they damaged the synagogue. Now they're throwing rocks at menorahs. But I can tell you this—we're going to do everything we can to stop them."

"Are you going to shoot them?"

"No, son. I don't like to use my gun—almost never do, as a matter of fact. I'm the kind of policeman who tries to help people without using guns and bullets."

Isaac was surprised. All the policemen he saw on TV seemed to shoot their guns a lot.

"Will you put them in jail?"

"If we can catch them, we will. But I think there's another way we can do something about this," Chief Inman answered, "and that's if the whole town takes a stand. I'm going to do what I can to make that happen.

"Now, tell me what you remember about the rock throwing . . ."

After Chief Inman and Mrs. Davis had left, Isaac and his parents sat at the kitchen table, drinking hot chocolate and talking.

"Chief Inman said that the people who threw the rock probably don't even *know* us!" Isaac exclaimed. "So why would they do it?"

"Just because we're Jewish," his dad answered. "They don't know anything about the kind of people that we are, and still they choose to hate us.

"It's the same with the other families in town they're trying to frighten. They don't know them, either, but they don't like their color or their religion or some of their beliefs."

"But *why*?" Isaac asked.

"I wish I knew," his dad said. "Haters and bullies have been around for as long as anyone can remember."

Isaac was quiet for a few moments. Then he burst out, "Let's put our menorahs away. Then maybe they won't bother us again."

His dad put his arm around him. "I know how you feel," he said. "It's frightening. But celebrating Hanukkah is part of being Jewish. It's what we believe in. We're not about to let some bullies keep us from celebrating our holiday."

"Dad's right, Isaac," his mom added. "We come from a family of pioneers. They came to Montana so they could do things their own way. In a sense, I guess, we're pioneers, too."

"But I don't want to be a pioneer," Isaac protested. "I want to be like everyone else."

"Sticking up for a belief is never easy," his dad said. "But we're not alone. A lot of people in this town—all kinds of people—are really angry at what these haters have been doing. And we're going to fight back. For one thing, Mom's decided to get in touch with the local TV stations. She wants to be interviewed so she can tell everyone in Billings what happened to us, and ask people to help."

"Mom's going to be on TV? Really?" Isaac asked excitedly.

"You know Mom," his dad said. "When something happens that she thinks is wrong, she speaks her mind."

Isaac rolled his eyes. "Yeah, that's Mom all right."

The next day, a television reporter and cameraman came to the Schnitzers' home. As the camera rolled, Isaac's mom explained what had happened the night before and spoke about the acts of hate toward other people in Billings.

Then she showed the reporter and cameraman Isaac's bedroom. Earlier, police detectives had come to take pictures and look for clues, so nothing had been moved.

That evening, Isaac was excited to see his room on the news, but he felt kind of funny, too. He had slept in his parents' bedroom the night before, but tonight he would be back in his own room again. Would he be safe? The Hanukkah decorations were still up in all the other windows, but he hadn't put his menorah back yet and he wasn't sure he wanted to. What if someone threw another rock?

He talked about this with his parents as they finished cleaning up his room. The broken window had been repaired, and Isaac's bed had been moved away from the window.

"We're going to do everything we can to protect you, Isaac," his mom reassured him. "Chief Inman has arranged to have the police keep a careful eye on our house, and our neighbors have promised that they're going to do the same."

"Whether or not you put your menorah back up is your choice," his dad said. "You take some time to think about it."

Isaac nodded. He still didn't know what to do.

Many people in Billings saw Mrs. Schnitzer on TV and had read about what was happening in the town newspaper. Then a special meeting was called by Chief Inman and a woman named Margaret MacDonald. She was a friend of the Schnitzers and had worked with many of the churches in Billings on special projects.

The day of the meeting was cold and blustery, but a big crowd filled the hall. Isaac and his parents were there, too.

"The police are doing everything they can to catch these people," Chief Inman told the crowd. "But it's important that we take a stand as a community. We have to show that an act of hate against even one person in Billings is an act of hate against all of us!"

"I have an idea," said Ms. MacDonald. "I've been thinking about a story my parents told me when I was a child. It's about what happened in Denmark during World War II. It was so inspiring that I've never forgotten it. This is what I remember:

During World War II, many countries in Europe were fighting the Nazis, who believed that Jews, and some other people, should be imprisoned or killed because they were different. The Nazis ordered Jews to sew stars on their clothing so they could be easily identified.

But Denmark had a courageous king named Christian. King Christian believed that the lives of all the Danish people were precious. According to legend, after the Nazis conquered Denmark, King Christian said that if the Jews had to wear stars, then he would wear one, too.

The next morning, when King Christian rode on horseback out of the palace, he was wearing a Jewish star. Soon many of the Danes were wearing them, too.

The Danes knew that the enemy had threatened to punish them if they tried to help their Jewish neighbors, but that didn't stop these brave people. Because they stood together against the Nazis, many Jews were saved.

"The Schnitzers have been urged to take down their menorahs so they won't be a target. But that's not the answer," continued Ms. MacDonald. "What if the rest of us were told to take down our Christmas trees and lights because people might throw rocks at us for being Christians? I say, let's take a stand like the Danish people did. Let's *all* put up menorahs."

"Great idea!" said Reverend Torney, who was the minister at the First Congregational Church. "I'll speak to the other religious leaders who couldn't come to the meeting today. Then we'll talk to our congregations."

"But where can we get menorahs?" someone asked.

"I think I have a solution," Reverend Torney answered. "Our Sunday school just had a lesson about Hanukkah, and we handed out pictures of menorahs to all the children. We'll make copies of the picture, and the churches can help distribute them throughout the town."

"Let's do it," called out Becky Thomas, a neighbor of the Schnitzers. Lots of others in the crowd shouted their agreement.

Reverend Torney smiled. The plan just might work.

The day after the meeting, Isaac's class talked about what had happened to Isaac and his family. Isaac's teacher, Mrs. Pearson, had asked Isaac to bring in his menorah and to explain why his family celebrated Hanukkah.

His friend Teresa Hanley had never seen a menorah. "What are the candles for?" she asked.

So Isaac told the class the story of Hanukkah.

Long ago, in the second century B.C., Israel was ruled by King Antiochus of Syria. He decreed that the Jews could no longer practice their religious traditions. This greatly angered them, and so a small group of freedom fighters, called the Maccabees, fought a three-year war against the Syrians. Though they were greatly outnumbered, the Maccabees fought heroically and were finally victorious.

After the war, according to legend, the Maccabees went to reclaim the Temple in Jerusalem and prepare it for worship. When they tried to light the sacred lamp at the Temple's altar, they found only one small jar of oil—just enough to provide light for a single night. But miraculously, the oil kept the lamp burning for eight nights.

That's why the menorah has nine candles. There is one for each night, with an extra candle to light the others. Every year Jews celebrate Hanukkah by lighting menorahs and remembering the victory of the Maccabees against religious intolerance.

"That's a wonderful story," said Mrs. Pearson.

"Some bullies threw a rock in the window where I had my menorah," Isaac blurted out, "just because I'm Jewish!"

"Were you scared?" Jonathan wanted to know.

"Well, maybe a little," Isaac admitted.

"That was a hard thing to have happened to you and your family," Mrs. Pearson said. "I read about it in the *Billings Gazette*, and so did the other teachers. We're all very sorry—and angry.

"Like Isaac said, Hanukkah celebrates the fight for religious freedom. The truth is, people have to fight this battle over and over again. We're doing it now in Billings.

"Has anyone else in the class ever been picked on for being different? Or do you know someone else to whom that happened?"

"I know someone," Teresa volunteered. "Last year there was a new boy in my class. His name is Caleb, and he's Cheyenne. He comes from the Reservation. Some of the kids didn't like that. They weren't very nice to him. So I tried to be his friend. I talked to him, and we played games together. Then the other kids started to play with him, too."

"Good for you!" Mrs. Pearson told her. "How did it feel when other kids started following your example?"

"It made me feel happy," Teresa answered.

"My sister has to use a wheelchair," Jeff said. "And some kids at school stare at her and tease her because she's different. They shouldn't do that. It hurts her feelings, and sometimes it makes her cry."

"Yes, that's very cruel," Mrs. Pearson said. "What do you think you would do if someone were bullying *you*?"

"Maybe I would go to another school," Jasmine answered.

"You might want to," said Mrs. Pearson, "but wouldn't that be a little like running away? It's just the opposite of standing up and saying to a bully, 'I won't let you push me around.'"

"Yeah—if you run away from bullies, they'll know you're scared and they'll push you around even more," said Matthew. "My dad told me that."

"He's absolutely right," Mrs. Pearson agreed. "That's why the town is taking a stand. Because when people stand up to bullies—especially when they stand up together—lots of times the bullies back down. And something else happens, too. The people who are being picked on know that they aren't alone. They know other people care.

"So some of us are going to be putting menorahs in our windows even though we're not Jewish. We want to show our support for Isaac's family and the other families that are being harassed in Billings."

Teresa liked the idea. She had been trying to imagine how she would feel if someone threw a rock into her window because she had a Christmas tree. It wasn't fair that Isaac had to have this happen to him! She knew she had to do something to help.

When Teresa came home from school that day, she told her mom what the class had talked about. "I want to have a menorah in *our* window, Mom. For Isaac," Teresa said.

"I've been thinking the same thing," her mom said. "But it's a decision we should make as a family. We've got to wait until everyone comes home. Then we'll all talk about this together."

It seemed like forever before Teresa's three sisters, her brother, and her father were home. Finally, as they ate their supper, the family talked about Teresa's idea.

"I don't know much about Hanukkah," Michael said.

"Me either," said Juliann.

Teresa told her family how Isaac had explained the holiday. The other children wanted to hear more, so they went to the encyclopedia and looked up the section about Hanukkah. Each child read a part aloud.

"This holiday's pretty neat," Michael said. "I like the part about the Maccabees."

In the encyclopedia was a picture of a menorah, just as Teresa had described it. "Let's draw our own menorah," she said, "and put it in the window."

"But what if people think we're Jewish?" Elizabeth asked.

"So what if they do?" Michael said.

"We could get a rock thrown through our window—that's what," said Elizabeth nervously. "Or maybe something worse."

"We *would* be taking a risk," Mr. Hanley said. "But some risks are worth it. People shouldn't be treated this way. What if this happened to us? Wouldn't we want people to help?"

"Count me in," Michael said.

"I'll do it," said Elizabeth.

Juliann and Kathleen agreed, too.

"Think of it like this," said Mrs. Hanley. "We never did like our living room windows much, anyway."

The family laughed. But they knew what they would do.

"Mom," Isaac called out as he walked in the door after gymnastics, "my friend Greg told me that the Catholic high school put a big sign in their window that said, 'Let's try to get along,' and someone threw a brick at it and smashed the window in a zillion pieces!"

"Yes, I know," his mom answered. "I was just at a meeting about it. As usual, those cowards did their dirty work in the dark, so they couldn't be seen. Thank goodness the school was empty, and no one was hurt."

"Is the school mad at us?" Isaac asked her.

"Honey, why would the school be mad at us? If they're mad at anyone, they would be mad at the person who threw the brick," his mother said.

"But they were sort of doing this for us, and now their window got smashed."

Isaac's mom thought for a moment before she answered. "Yes, Isaac, they're doing it for us. And for the other families that these haters are trying to scare. But they're doing it for themselves, too. They're trying to make Billings a better place to live—for everyone."

Then Isaac's mom had an idea. "Don't take your coat off. We're going out for a drive."

"Where?" Isaac asked, surprised. It was almost time for dinner.

"You'll see."

It was getting dark as Isaac and his mother began to drive slowly through the neighborhood.

"Look, Mom!" Isaac cried. "Look at all the menorahs!" In house after house, in the frosty windows, Isaac could see pictures of menorahs. There wasn't a single street without the Hanukkah symbols.

"Like our house," Isaac said.

"That's right," his mother agreed.

"Did anyone else have rocks thrown through their windows?" Isaac asked.

"Yes, they did," his mom answered. "But you know what?"

Isaac shook his head.

"People have become even more determined. The *Billings Gazette* printed a full-page picture of a menorah and asked people to display it on a door or window in their homes. And they did, Isaac—people put up thousands of menorahs."

Isaac was silent for a bit, thinking. Then he said, slowly, "Mom, remember last year when I told you I wanted to bring some of my Hanukkah presents to school to show the other guys?"

"Uh-huh," his mom answered.

"Well . . . now don't be mad . . . but I didn't tell them they were Hanukkah presents. I felt funny, Mom. Nobody else gets Hanukkah presents. Everyone gets presents for *Christmas*. And I didn't want to be different. I just wanted to be like the rest of the class."

"So what did you do?"

"Uh . . . I guess I sort of told them that they were Christmas presents. But not this year, Mom," he added quickly. "This time, when I show my presents, I'm going to say I got them for Hanukkah."

"I'm glad, Isaac," his mom answered softly.

"Mom, stop!" Isaac suddenly shouted.

"What is it?" she asked, slamming on the brakes.

"Look!"

Ahead was a house with a big picture window. Taped onto the window was a large picture of a beautiful menorah drawn with many brightly colored crayons. Over the menorah was a message. "For our friend Isaac," it read, "with love from Teresa and the rest of the Hanley family." Underneath was a picture of a Jewish star and a Christian cross.

"She didn't tell me she was doing this," Isaac said. "She never said anything . . ."

Isaac's mom turned toward him, and he saw there were tears in her eyes.

"You know, honey, hate can make a lot of noise. Love and courage are usually quieter. But in the end, they're the strongest."

All the way home, Isaac looked at the menorahs in his neighbors' windows. He thought about what his mom had said. And then he made a decision.

The next day was gray and gloomy. But in the evening, a warm, inviting light shone from Isaac's bedroom. Gathered around the window were Isaac and all the Hanley children. They had just finished putting up new holiday decorations.

Isaac's menorah was perched on the sill. Each branch was brightly lit and shone on the sign which had been strung across the length of the window. "Happy Hanukkah to everyone in Billings," the sign read, "with love, Isaac."

As Hanukkah passed and Christmas grew nearer, more and more menorahs could be seen throughout Billings. The town continued to fight against the acts of hatred, and slowly but surely those acts began to stop. The townspeople told each other this was a gift they had given to themselves. And that it was their best holiday gift, ever.

I have received so much help and encouragement with this book that it is impossible to properly thank everyone in this limited space. Those closest to me understand, and know who they are. I do, however, want to acknowledge my indebtedness to the following people:

Jane Marks, a wonderful writer and friend, who originally conceived of this project and provided crucial help, support, and direction.

Dr. Marvin Goldstein, who helped clarify the true story of how the Danish people helped save their Jewish fellow citizens from the Nazis.

All the third graders of the Burnt Hill Road School, in Montgomery Township, New Jersey, who acted as literary critics upon being read early versions of the text in 1994. I have used many of their ideas.

Jane Clarke Fowkes, Bill Fowkes, and their daughters Laura and Julia, who read each version of the manuscript and provided critical suggestions.

My editor, Kathy Tucker, who lavished so much care and attention to detail on this book it's hard to imagine how it could have been done without her.

And Newark Beth Israel Medical Center, most particularly Paula Sabreen, A.C.S.W., and Stuart Rosenthal, M.S., M.D., of the Department of Psychiatry, and Aron Schlam, senior vice-president of the Medical Center, who provided unstinting encouragement. Their efforts helped make it possible for me to draw upon the Medical Center's considerable resources to get the story of Billings told.   J.C.

Library of Congress Cataloging-in-Publication Data

Cohn, Janice.
      The Christmas menorahs: how a town fought hate / Janice Cohn;
illustrations by Bill Farnsworth.
      p. cm.
      Summary: Describes how people in Billings, Montana, joined together to fight a series of hate crimes.
      ISBN 0-8075-1152-8
1. Jews–Montana–Billings–Juvenile literature. 2. Anti-Semitism-Montana–Billings–Juvenile literature.
3. Hate crimes–Montana–Billings–Juvenile literature. 4. Hanukkah–Juvenile literature. 5. Billings
(Mont.)–Ethnic relations–Juvenile literature.
[1. Prejudices. 2. Anti-Semitism. 3. Hate crimes. 4. Hanukkah.] I. Farnsworth, Bill, ill. II. Title.
F739.B5C64   1995   95-2053
305.892'4078639–dc20   CIP
                                                        AC

Design by Lucy Smith.
The text of this book is set in Bauer Bodoni.
The illustrations are rendered in oil paint.